ABOUT THE AUTHOR

Despite having written extensively for radio, television, publishing and the theatre, Alistair Beaton has never before ventured into the field of complete bollocks. He has found it a deeply meaningful, life-altering experience.

Alistair Beaton lives in North London without a psychotherapist.

D1026464

NEW BEGINNINGS

Break through to a whole new life in less
than a day.

Here's how:

Buy ten self-help books.

Take them home.

Put them in a pile on the floor.

Sit on them.

Watch television.

BLUE

The sky is blue for a reason.

Blue light is a source of strength and harmony in the cosmos.

Create a blue light in your life by telephoning the police.

IN TOUCH

Get in touch with yourself by
touching yourself.

If somebody is watching,
stop touching yourself.

MISSION STATEMENT

Have a T-shirt made with your personal
mission statement on it.

Wear it to parties.

Feels good, doesn't it?

But can your whole life be summed up
in a T-shirt?

No! You're a bigger person than that!

You'd better have *two* T-shirts!

SENSES

Deal with your inner stress by indulging your senses: look for a rainbow, stroke a piece of silk, listen to a cat purring, sniff a newly-cut rose.

If no one is around, do drugs.

PROFOUND

The inner self is only the outer self turned
inside out.
Light a candle and think about this.

YOUR ANGER

Remember that anger can be your friend. Talk to your anger. Give your anger a soothing cup of sage and lemon tea. Take your anger out for a walk with you. Buy your anger a new pullover. Explain to your anger that you have needs, too. Don't be afraid to shout back at your anger. (Ask your heart to be the referee). Once your anger sees sense, reward it by bingeing on chocolate digestives. Before you go to bed, give your anger a hug.

GETTING OLDER

Most string instruments improve with age.

Think of yourself as a violin, growing more melodious and resonant with every passing year.

Then think of yourself being picked up and handled by some raddled musician with thinning hair and bad teeth.

Don't think about this any more.

SIMPLE PLEASURES

Make room for flowers in your life. On your way home from work, buy a single daffodil, put it in a vase on your kitchen table, and sit silently for the whole evening, contemplating the beauty of the flower while absorbing its precious Yang energy. To heighten your pleasure, sip from a glass of home-made barley water. Round the evening off with a bowl of boiled buckwheat sprinkled with nourishing sesame seeds. As you go to bed, give yourself a hug.

If you still feel sad, try line-dancing.

INNER GARDENING

Your mind is a garden, and like a garden it needs your love and attention.

Mow the garden of your mind on a regular basis and pull out weeds whenever they appear. If your neighbour uses a strimmer, ask if you can borrow it.
(Be careful to avoid unwanted lobotomies.)

JUST A THOUGHT

Seek beauty in a raindrop, but
buy a new coat.

A TIP

Never underestimate the healing
powers of custard.

CLOTHES AND YOU

The clothes you wear reveal a great deal about the sort of person you are.

Surprise other people by taking all your clothes off before you go out.

HAVE A LAUGH

Laughter is often the best medicine.
Find a person much poorer than you, and
laugh at them.

PAIN

Confront your pain by drawing a picture of it.

Hang it on the wall in a prominent position.

Invite friends to your home to look at it.

Ask them to tell you what it says to them.

If people stop coming to your home, share your pain with your cat instead.

RAW SYNERGY

Harness the natural synergy of raw vegetables in order to purge your body of toxins. The more raw vegetables you eat in combination, the more powerful will be the purging. Try the potent combination of raw onions, raw beets, raw potatoes, raw celeriac, raw leeks, raw parsnips, raw sorrel and raw Chinese artichokes. This combination is particularly efficacious the night before a major stress-event, such as an exam or interview, since it means you will be too ill to attend it.

GRIEVING

There is no such thing as inappropriate grief. Losing a friend can lead to feelings of great sadness.
Losing a sock can also be distressing.

In the same way that you make space to mourn your friends, make space to mourn your socks.

REVOLUTION

Political revolution is easy. Spiritual revolution is hard.

By fighting to free yourself from childhood trauma, you are fighting for a spiritual revolution, which is the only true means of change.

Be proud – you are a freedom fighter!

(Try to avoid the word *'terrorist'*.)

QUALITY TIME

Stressed by the pressures of bringing up a family? Enhance your parenting skills by making quality time for yourself.

Lay aside three to four hours every evening when you can sit alone in a room and read, listen to music, or meditate.

Before you start, leave the children in front of a video with an organic baked potato. Explain that you cannot be there for them unless you are there for yourself.

If the children develop disruptive behaviour patterns, seek the help of a child psychiatrist. (You might also consider having them adopted.)

MAKING SPACE

Make space for yourself by getting rid of the clutter in your life:

Throw away your unwanted clothes

Burn your old files

Clear out the rubbish in your attic

Dispose of your grandmother.

PLUCK IT

On your way home from work, pluck a leaf from a tree. Examine it. What shape is it? What colour is it? Ask yourself, what life experiences has this leaf been through?

Pluck another leaf. Look at it. Ask yourself, what journey has this leaf made?

Pluck a third leaf, turn it over in your hand. Ask yourself, why do I feel unconditional love for this leaf?

Go home. Get a life.

BEYOND WORDS

Understand the importance of non-verbal messaging. Give people the sound cues which reveal your mood:

If you are happy, ululate in people's ears

If you are anxious, make moaning noises

If you are depressed, fart loudly and persistently.

Basically, fuck all.

(answer to question on previous page)

THE BUMBLEBEE

Sit in a park on a warm summer's day and watch a bumblebee go from flower to flower. What can you learn from the bumblebee?

NON-JUDGMENTAL

Learn to be non-judgmental about yourself.
If you lose your temper and punch someone
in the teeth, don't torture yourself with
feelings of guilt. Instead, observe yourself
carefully next time you're punching someone
in the teeth, and ask yourself, 'What is it
about the other person that makes me want
to punch them in the teeth?'
Enter into a dialogue with the other person,
helping them to come to terms with their
unacknowledged feelings of aggression
towards you.
If they refuse to enter into a dialogue with
you, punch them in the teeth again.

OWNERSHIP

Your body belongs to you and not to anyone else. Don't let anyone borrow it unless you want it to be borrowed.

If someone does borrow it, insist that they bring it back on time.

MEN
and
WOMEN
are
different

(See also, by the same author,
Men are from Bars, Women have no Penis,
published by Bollocks Books Ltd, price £9.99.)

FEELINGS

Do you find your emotional flow blocked by unwanted pain?

Unblock your flow by asking a friend to be your feelings facilitator.

If your friend refuses, release your emotions by screaming loudly for ten minutes.

Afterwards, write a loving letter to your friend, explaining in a non-judgmental way why you feel let down.

LOVE

Love is not just a feeling, love is a powerful tool. Show your powerful tool to people and ask them to admire it. If they don't want to look at it, put it away again.

EXPLORING

The biggest and most exciting region
left to discover is the unknown territory of
your mind.

Explore your mind.

(Leave a note with a friend or neighbour
with details of where you're heading.)

MORE DEPRESSION

Sometimes, when you're depresssed, you feel
you're going to be depressed for ever. This is
an illusion. You won't be depressed after
you're dead. *

* As far as we know.

UNCONDITIONAL LOVE

You are the only person who
loves you unconditionally.

You are the only person who accepts
you absolutely.

You are the only person who wants to be
with you twenty-four hours a day.

You are the only person who wants to
look in your handkerchief after you've
blown your nose.

Congratulations! You are probably the most
tolerant person you will ever meet!

LETTING GO

Let go of your fear.
Let go of your tension.
Let go of your inhibitions.
Let go of your job.
Let go of your husband.
Let go of your wife.
Let go of your parents.
Let go of your children.
Let go of your home.
Let go of your money.
Let everything go!

(Talk to a friend before embarking on this.)

DIRT

Have you ever wondered why the Dyson vacuum cleaner has become so popular?

Could it be because you can actually see the dirt you've removed from your home?

When you're clearing out your inner debris, don't just vacuum up your negative feelings, Dyson them!

(If what you're clearing out is too horrible to look at, ask a friend with seeing difficulties to do your Dysoning for you.)

CHILLY

Do you ever catch yourself staring aimlessly
into the fridge?

If so, remember this:

You may find butter in your fridge.

You may find cheese in your fridge.

You may find vegetables in your fridge.

But you will not find answers in your fridge.

Instead thank your fridge for the
gift of coolness.

SELF-ESTEEM

Feeling bad about yourself? You're probably suffering from low self-esteem.

Give your self-esteem a boost by making lots of delicious rhubarb jam.

EMBRACE THE WORLD

Live once in Paris.

Live once in Rio.

Live once in Bogota.

(It's generally considered wise to
do Bogota last.)

BLOCKS

Feeling tired and listless?
Your energy is being blocked by
energy blocks.

Find new energy by unblocking your
energy blocks.

Once your energy blocks are unblocked, try
to find out why you were experiencing
energy blocks in the first place.

If you don't have the energy to find out why
you were experiencing energy blocks in the
first place, it could be that your energy is
being blocked by new energy blocks.

At this point it's probably best to give up.

BEFORE BREAKFAST

Ten minutes of Mongolian Vibration
Chanting before breakfast will do wonders
for your skin tone.

SIMPLE PLEASURES

Get pleasure out of the little things in life.
Stand on an ant.

GENDER

If you find yourself constantly hitting your partner over the head with a heavy iron frying pan, you may be deficient in essential gender conflict resolution skills.

Hone your gender conflict resolution skills by giving your partner a warning thwack on the shins before hitting them over the head.

HUMAN POTENTIAL

Realise your full human potential by going
on a Cranio-Sacral Therapy Weekend.

CLOSURE

Unresolved issues in the workplace can
be a source of great tension for you
and your colleagues.

Achieve closure by slamming a door in the
face of somebody less important than you.

E-MAIL

Choose an e-mail address that reflects your
true self.

Here's one suggestion:

I.am@one.with.myself

YIN AND YANG

Your psychic energy is divided into
Yin and Yang.

Most people are either
mostly Yin or mostly Yang.

Yin is the channeller.

Yang is the healer.

If you want to channel your healing, get your
Yin to talk to your Yang.

If you want to heal your channels, get your
Yang to talk to your Yin.

If you want to experience psychic peace, tell
them both to shut up.

RESPECT

Your parents are older than you.

Treat them with respect.

Ask them to give you the same respect as you give them.

If they fail to do this, check out the old people's homes in your area.

Let your parents know you're doing this.

They'll quickly become more attuned to your emotional needs.

GETTING IN TOUCH
WITH THE REAL YOU

Make sure you are entirely
alone in the house.

Stand in a circle.

Hold hands with yourself.

Write a letter to yourself.

Phone yourself.

Talk to yourself.

Shoot yourself.

CONFIDENCE

Before that important work meeting boost
your confidence by reading a few pages from
The Tibetan Book of the Dead.

FIRST DATE

Going on a first date? Before you leave the house, give your immune system a boost by eating lots of raw garlic.

ON THE PLANE

During long air journeys, endear yourself to crew and passengers alike by introducing those around you to the ancient power of group chant.

BELIEF IN YOURSELF

Never lose belief in yourself. Every morning, stand in front of your bathroom mirror and say to yourself, 'I am talented and beautiful. People adore me. I am popular because I deserve to be popular.' Repeat this ten times.

Don't tell anyone you're doing this – nobody wants to be friends with a sad bastard who talks to himself in mirrors.

KEEP THEM INFORMED

Nurture your friendships by sending out a monthly round robin to all those who love and cherish you for who you are.

Include details of your bowel movements.

IN THE KITCHEN

When preparing a meal, be sure to establish
a positive relationship with your ingredients:

Respect your bean-shoots

Empathise with your aubergines

Enter into a dialogue with your marrow

Get feedback from your fennel

But don't take any crap from your artichokes.

Now open your eyes and look in the mirror – you will be amazed to catch sight of an attractive and successful person.

Call the police and tell them an attractive and successful person has broken into your bedroom.

VISUALISATION

Before going to bed at night, take all your clothes off and stand in front of your bedroom mirror.

Relax, close your eyes, and breathe deeply.

Now visualise yourself walking along a beautiful sandy beach.

You see an attractive and successful person coming out of the water.

The attractive and successful person is also completely naked.

You realise the attractive and successful person is YOU!

SIMPLICITY

If you feel stale and depressed, try buying less. At first you'll find it difficult, but gradually you'll be able to buy so little that your standard of living will be the same as that of an Indian villager. Experience the simplicity of extreme poverty for three days. Start buying again.

THE MOMENT

Stress and conflict come from thinking too much about the future.

Whenever possible, cherish the moment, possess the moment, stay in the moment. If there's a large clock around, open it up and get inside.

ACHIEVING

Each morning, write down ten useful things that you would like to achieve that day. At the end of the day, look at the list. If you haven't achieved any of your ten aims, throw the list away and write instead a list of ten completely useless things you did that day. Now put a tick opposite each of them. Pin this list on your bedroom wall, and fall asleep secure in the knowledge that you are an achiever.

REMEMBER

You are the most important person you will
ever meet.

Why not ask yourself for an autograph?

*(Tell yourself, it's not for you,
it's for your inner child.)*

LOSS OF PARTNER

If your partner dies, ease your grief by
starting a herb garden.

RESPECTING YOUR FEET

Your feet deserve more love than they get.
Make your feet feel loved and needed by
soaking them in a mixture of warm aloe vera
juice, jojoba cream, liquidised artichoke
hearts and tea tree oil. Afterwards, make a
delicious and nourishing soup with it, and
invite your friends round to share this
affirmation of your uniqueness.

SAYING YES

Learn to say 'yes' to yourself. If yourself gets too demanding, learn to say:

'We'll see',

or

'Not right now',

or

'Maybe later'.

SADNESS

Sadness is a bad place to be. Happiness is a good place to be.

To get out of the bad place, leave it, and go to the good place instead.

There may not be a bus service running between the bad place and the good place, so be prepared for a long walk.

If your partner feels threatened by your legitimate need for self-exploration, explain that you need to be at one with yourself before you can be at one with anyone else.

When you hear the front door slam, call out to your ex-partner, thanking them for understanding your need for personal space.

SETTING LIMITS

Your partner will only truly respect you if you set limits.

Make your boundaries clear.

Explain to your partner that they must seek permission before touching you intimately.

Assert your need for personal space by painting a black line down the middle of the bed.

Affirm your specialness by asking your partner to look after the cat while you spend your summer holiday in a Zen monastery or inter-faith retreat.

DYSFUNCTIONAL

A dysfunctional family is not a family that fails to function; a dysfunctional family is a family that fails to function for *you*.

Make your family function for you by asking family members to rub essential oils into your thighs. If anyone refuses, ask them why they feel threatened by your thighs.

PAINFUL

Make space for pain in your life.

If you feel just fine, seek out a counsellor or therapist who will explore with you the reasons why you are denying your pain.

THE MUSIC OF LIFE

Let your life be filled with music.

Install a speaker in your bathroom, so you can listen to your favourite CD in the bath. Take a Walkman or portable CD player with you when you travel. Listen to the harmony of the spheres while shopping. Sing extracts from La Bohème to the checkout girl at Tesco's. Hum your favourite tune while eating in a restaurant. Whistle cheerfully during sexual intercourse.

MAKING PEACE WITH TECHNOLOGY

Programme your video with love.

Change your channels with compassion.

Talk to your answering machine.

Make love to your CD-Rom drive.

(Switch the power off first.)

TOO BUSY

Your mind is like a motorway. Sometimes it can be jammed by too much traffic. Avoid the jams by never using your mind on a Bank Holiday weekend.

YOUR TRUE FEELINGS

Getting in touch with your true feelings is like learning to swim – once you have learned how to do it, you will never forget.

Of course, if there are sharks around, knowing how to swim isn't going to help you much.

Similarly, before you embark on a long-term relationship, run a few checks on yourself:

Have I filled up my tank with love?

Can I see my way ahead?

Have I pumped up my commitment to the right level?

Are all my moving parts fully lubricated?

Ought I to take a shower first?

CHECK IT OUT

Before going on a long car journey, you do some basic checks:

Is the tank full of gas?

Are the lights working?

Are the tyres at the right pressure?

Is there enough oil to make the engine run smoothly?

Is the windscreen washer working?

YOUR FEELINGS OR THEIRS?

Without knowing it, you may be ascribing to other people the feelings you are experiencing yourself.

Because you hate yourself, you think other people hate you.

This is known as *projection*.

Sometimes, of course, other people really do hate you.

This is known as *hatred*.

There's not much you can do about it.

You're probably just the sort of person that people hate.

BEING YOU

It's okay to be you.

It's not okay to be somebody else.

Spare a thought for all those people who are somebody else.

It must be just *awful* for them!

NATURAL SELECTION

Nature offers you choices.

You can frolic with the dolphins or bask with the sharks.

Which would you rather do?

Why?

Write down your answer on a piece of paper and throw it into the sea.

If there's a litter bin near the beach, throw it into the litter bin instead.

HEALING POWER

Have you considered harnessing the healing
power of the cosmos?

No? Then go out and harness it now!

SHARING

Don't know what to do with your life?

Why not share it with a budgie or other animal companion?

A six-rod wind chime or a crystal can also be excellent company – what's more, both can be left for long periods on their own!

CONNECTING WITH OTHERS

Connect with others by gluing your forehead
to somebody else's.

UTTER PEACE

Lay aside one day a month as your very own
Day of Stillness.

Close the curtains.

Take the phone off the hook.

Don't read books or newspapers.

Don't eat or drink anything.

Don't watch TV.

Don't listen to the radio.

Don't do anything!

(It's okay to pick your nose a little)

FORGIVENESS

Forgiveness can be fun.

Throw a forgiveness party for the person who has done you wrong.

With your friends as witnesses, hold hands with your former enemy and say goodbye to your anger.

Get your friends to shout 'Goodbye anger!'

Throw a funeral party for your lost anger.

PHYSICAL HARMONY

Each organ of your body has a vital part to
play in your well-being. Make sure all your
organs work in harmony together. Make your
heart talk to your head. Get your pancreas to
chat to your liver. Invite your gall-bladder to
e-mail your ovaries.

If your lower intestine receives anonymous
calls, you should see a doctor immediately.

SATISFYING

Satisfy your inner child by eating ten
tubes of Smarties.

After seven to eight hours, the face in the mirror will suddenly become distorted and appear to be screaming. Do not be alarmed – this is perfectly normal.

Persist.

After eight to ten hours the face in the mirror will come to meet yours. It will feel as if you are bashing your head repeatedly into a glass object.

You will now find yourself in an altered state of consciousness.

This is known as *unconsciousness*.

It is followed by another, higher state, known as *hospital*.

MIRROR MEDITATION

Sit down in the lotus position, facing
a full-length mirror.

In complete silence, stare at your own face in
the mirror, without blinking.

For three or four hours,
nothing will happen.

Persist.

After four to six hours, the eyes of the face in
the mirror will start to roll its eyes and its
tongue will flop out of its mouth.

Do not be alarmed – this is perfectly normal.

Persist.

PETS

Show your animal companion your
appreciation by taking him or her with you
on your next tantric studies weekend.

GIBBERISH

To cleanse your mind of verbal accretions, and to deconstruct unnecessary verbalisations, talk gibberish for at least twenty minutes every day.

Don't be embarrassed if friends and colleagues can't understand what you're saying. Turn it into a game – see if they can guess when you're talking gibberish and when you're talking normally!

GETTING THE MOST OUT OF LIFE

Get the most out of life by
becoming very rich.

KIND WORDS

We often forget how hard life can be for an office junior or some other young person in the place where we work.

When people make mistakes, it doesn't always help to reproach them for it.

In fact, you'll be astonished how encouraging a few kind words can be.

After all, you don't have to mean them.

INFIDELITY

Sometimes, what we perceive as sexual infidelity is merely a reaffirmation of our essential humanity.

If you have been unfaithful to your partner, be completely honest and open – explain to your partner the circumstances and how you feel now.

If you've been reaffirming your essential humanity with large numbers of people, it might be best to get your partner to attend an anger management course before you go into all the details.

TRUST

Trust your feelings.

Give them space to express themselves.

Let them go out to the shops on their own.

But tell them not to take sweets
from strangers.

BE PRACTICAL

Use transcendent harmonics and resonance healing techniques to get your shoes repaired.

VIRUS

Your computer's crashed? Your hard disk may be suffering from a cosmic imbalance, or 'virus'. Restore your computer to health by taking the following steps:

1. Place a healing crystal on top of your VDU

2. Clear your PC's negative aura by lighting a joss stick

3. Reinvigorate your mouse by massaging it with essential oils

4. Energise your CD Rom drive by intoning ancient Hindu mantras

5. Buy a new computer.

APPEARANCES

You don't really need make-up.

Celebrate your authentic face by frightening people on the street.

BEING ALONE

Loneliness is only the absence of
other people.

You are alone because you choose
to be alone.

Those people across the road having a great
party are only projecting their loneliness on
to other people. Spare a thought for the
emptiness of their lives as you curl up snugly
with a mug of fennel tea and a copy of
The Little Book of Calm.

MIDLIFE CRISIS

If you are a male aged between forty and fifty, you may experience a sudden loss of libido.
Don't panic.
Ask your secretary if she's seen it.
Check under the sofa.
Report your loss to the police.
Consider offering a reward for the safe return of your libido. If, after six months there is still no sign of it, take up gardening.

YOUR BODY

Your body is a superb instrument.

Why not invite it to join an orchestra?

TRAVEL PLANS

Planning to travel? Why not stay at home, and go on a beautiful meditation journey instead?

It's cheaper, it's more fulfilling, and you won't have to meet other people!

ALLERGIES

Don't condemn others for their actions unless you know the cause. That masked man waving a gun in the bank may just be having an allergic reaction to pollen.

INDULGE YOURSELF

We can't be sensible all the time.
Every now and then, throw caution to the
wind and buy yourself twice as much tofu as
you really need!

ROAD RAGE

To avoid succumbing to road rage, close your
eyes and imagine you are lying in a beautiful
meadow on a summer's day.
Touch the blades of grass.
Smell the wild flowers.
See the butterflies flitting past.
Hear the sound of tearing metal as you drive
into the car in front of you.

WAR AND PEACE

Help end world conflict by building a peace
pagoda for your pet.

COLOUR THERAPY

Try painting your therapist a different colour.

EMPTINESS

Let emptiness be your friend.
Empty your mind.
Empty your bank account.
Empty a bottle.

THE INNER CORE

Lie down in a grassy park and
relax completely.

Close your eyes.

Access your deep inner core by listening to
your breathing.

After a few minutes, you will find yourself
suffused by a feeling of warmth.

Check to see whether you've been pissed on
by a dog.

WIND

If the noise from your neighbour's wind chime becomes oppressive, ring your local council and ask them to send round the Feng Shui Control Officer.

JOURNEYS

Going on a long flight? Make it a unique
transformational journey by changing into
fresh underwear while still on the plane.

EASY AS PIE

Make a pie chart of your love.

How big a slice is devoted to YOU?

Is the slice big enough?

Why not give yourself an extra slice?

Better still, why not give yourself the entire pie!

SURFING

You could surf the Net for a thousand years and still not find the web site that speaks to *you*.

Surf your inner net for five minutes every night and you will always find a web site that will give you the attention you deserve.

It'll probably look something like this:

www.me.com

STRESSED OUT

Stressed out? Go outside, lie down on your back, spread your arms and legs in an X-shape and stare up at the sky. Stay in that position until you can feel your connection to the infinite. If you hear the rumble of approaching traffic, you may be lying in the middle of a road. Ask the infinite if you could call back later.

FAILURE

Failure is only success waiting to happen.

Next time you feel you're a failure, just say to yourself, 'I'm waiting to happen!'

PAMPER YOUR NOSE

Just think what your nose goes through
in the course of a day – dirt, dust,
pollution, fumes.

When you get home from a day in town,
pamper your nose in all kinds of ways:

Burn a joss stick

Expose your nose to the fragrance of
essential oils

Let your system absorb vital bio-flavonoids
by inserting an organic cherry tomato
into each nostril.

MAKING THE LEAP

The old you is only the new you waiting
to be undressed.

Or vice versa.

REPETITIVE STRESS SYNDROME

Thinking of others can be very stressful.
If you think of others all the time you
may become a victim of repetitive
stress syndrome.

Avoid this danger by thinking about
yourself as much as possible.

NEVER TOO LATE

Does it feel too late to change your life? If so,
put all the clocks in the house back by at
least three hours. Now use those extra hours
to change your life.

BEATING THE BLUES

Depression is only a problem if you decide that it's a problem. If you decide it's a comfortable old jacket, you'll find you can put it on or take it off whenever you feel like it. Then when you feel ready, you can take your depression to the Oxfam shop and pass it on to someone in the Third World.

VICTIM

You are a victim because you believe you
don't deserve anything better.

It doesn't always have to be this way.

Let somebody else be a victim for a change.

Next time you're walking down a busy street,
push somebody else under a bus and shout,
'Look, a victim, and it's somebody else!'

Deal with any residual guilt feelings by using
Reiki healing techniques.

HIGHS & LOWS

We talk of 'the height of folly' and 'the depths of despair'.

Yet why is folly high?

And why is despair deep?

Challenge conventional wisdom: experience the depths of folly and the heights of despair!

SPRING CLEANING

Spring clean your mind. Brush away the
cobwebs of guilt. Scrub out the stains of
anxiety. Hoover up the dust of depression.
Take your brain to the dry cleaners.
(Don't lose the ticket.)

URINE

Let urine be the mirror of your soul.
Every Monday morning, use a chopstick*
to whisk a little of your urine in a white
porcelain bowl. If your urine turns frothy,
you have a terminal illness and will be dead
by the weekend.

* If you have issues around chopsticks,
it is better to use a fork.

SHARING A HOME

Loving another person does not necessarily
mean putting the other person first.
Authentic love is the love of another,
co-existing in perfect balance with
the love of self.

Help maintain that balance by not bothering
to empty the bath after you've used it.

DEPRESSION

Share your depression with other people by giving your depression a name. You might, for instance, decide to call it 'Herbert'. Then, when a friend calls to invite you out to dinner, you should enquire, 'Can Herbert come too?' If your friend is non-supportive, just say something like, 'I'm sorry, if you can't accept that I'm in a relationship with Herbert, then I really don't want to come to dinner with you.'

Another way of dealing with your depression is to give it a less depressing name than Herbert.

ECSTATIC

Experience pure ecstasy by running through a meadow of wild Alpine flowers. If there isn't a meadow of wild Alpine flowers in your area, try running across your back lawn. (Prolong the ecstasy by running very slowly.)

DEATH

Do not be afraid of death. Death is merely
the continuance of life, only without the
breathing. Eat lots of spinach.

NEGATIVE FEELINGS

When you have negative feelings, write them down on a piece of paper. Then hold the paper above a lighted candle. As you watch the flame consume the paper, say to yourself, 'Goodbye negative feelings.' Then go to the front door, throw it wide open, and exclaim, 'Hello, positive feelings, come on in!'

If you find there are no positive feelings on your doorstep at that particular moment, scream out loudly,

**'YOU BASTARDS,
YOU'RE SUPPOSED TO BE HERE!'**

FINDING OUT WHO YOU ARE

The best way to find out who you are is to go
up to somebody who knows who you are
and say, 'Hello, who am I?'

Looking at your name in a driving licence or
passport is another useful way of finding out
who you are.

THE CHILD WITHIN

Finding the child within yourself can be harder than you think. Buy a cuddly toy and take it to bed with you. Use it to rediscover the child-self you thought you had lost forever. Keep in touch with this child-self wherever you go. Throw tantrums with people who won't let you have your way. Eat too much chocolate and be sick. Show your partner your anger by wetting the bed.

CHANGE

Embrace change. But don't get into heavy
petting with it.

THE FUNNY SIDE

Enhance your relationship by always laughing at your partner's little jokes.

If your partner's little jokes aren't funny, laugh at his little penis instead.

INNER PEACE

Find inner peace by clenching and
unclenching your buttocks at least twenty
times a day.

CREATIVITY

Explore your creativity in new ways.
Paint a picture.
Compose a symphony.
Write a novel.
Direct a movie.
Build a bridge.
Construct a ten-lane highway.
Re-point the Great Wall of China.
Make a cup of tea.

TIRED AND SLUGGISH?

Tiredness and sluggishness can often be traced back to digestive problems.

Make room in your life for your large intestine. Give it some attention. Ask if it would be interested in colonic irrigation. Talk to your bottom about it. Listen to your bottom before taking a decision.

STRESS IN THE WORKPLACE

When you are experiencing stress in the workplace, there is nothing more soothing than a herbal tea. Make the tea in a large mug, add a generous spoonful of organic honey, then pour the contents over the desktop PC of the person who's been getting up your nose.

YOU CAN DO IT

Think of your negative feelings as
fruits or vegetables.

Your sadness is a tomato.

Your anxiety is a marrow.

Your guilt is a cucumber.

Crush the tomato. Squash the marrow.
Sit on the cucumber.

YOU

You are the most important person in your
life. Be as kind to yourself as you are
to other people.
Give yourself treats:
invite yourself out to dinner;
send yourself life-affirming e-mails;
ask yourself to share a holiday villa in Italy
with you; leave little love letters for yourself
around the house where you can discover
them by chance while you're doing
the hoovering; ask yourself to come with you
when you start your psychotherapy.

IMPORTANT

Feelings of unimportance are often caused by a lack of importance.

Banish your feelings of unimportance by becoming President of the United States.

This little book is dedicated with love
and sincerity to you, the reader.

Thank you for trusting me enough to
let me share my bollocks with you.

Let this little book be our
journey together:

A journey into the self

A journey into the beautiful light

A journey into complete bollocks.

BOLLOCKS (bol´-luks) n.pl. and n. sing. a profound insight, a revelation into the meaning of our lives. Literally, 'beautiful light' [Fr. beau, belle — Lat. bellus, fine, beautiful, + Lat. lux – light].

Later corrupted into meaning a nonsensical statement, a statement without meaning or substance. [O.E. beallucas, testicles. (vulg.)]

In this book the reader is offered a glimpse of the beautiful light which she or he may for too long have mistakenly assumed to be nothing but bollocks.